Assessing Communication

Clare Latham and Ann Miles
The Redway School

JAY

David Fulton Publishers
London

David Fulton Publishers Ltd
Ormond House, 26–27 Boswell Street, London WC1N 3JD

First published in Great Britain by The Redway School 1996
Published in 1997 by David Fulton Publishers Ltd

Note: The right of Clare Latham and Ann Miles to be identified as authors of their work has been asserted by them in accordance with the Copyright, Designs and Patents Act 1988.

Copyright © The Redway School

British Library Cataloguing in Publication Data
A catalogue record for this book is available from the British Library

ISBN 1–85346–503–8

Typeset by Sheila Knight
Printed in Great Britain by Bell and Bain Ltd Glasgow

Assessing Communication

Contents

Foreword

Barry Carpenter

Communication is not only central to the curriculum for children with severe and profound learning difficulties, it is central to their quality of life. The ability to exercise some control over their environment, and to initiate and receive communicative interactions, is fundamental to their development. However, the means of communication may be significantly different from conventional methods.

Pat Fitton (1994), in writing about the communications of her daughter Kathy (who had profound and multiple learning difficulties), highlights the many and various means of communications used:

> Kathy communicated with us by eye contact and a facial language of frowns, bad looks, smiles and raised eyebrows. She had a range of angry, unhappy or joyful sounds. She leaned towards objects and activities she wanted, or reached over in the desired direction. (p. 15)

How do teachers interpret any of these gestures? How can they be sure of the communicative intent embodied in the angry sounds, the eye flickering, the change in body posture? The assessment of communication in children with massive communication impairments is a major challenge. The significantly different patterns of communicative development in children with SLD/PMLD necessitates detailed observation and assessment to establish any reliable or valid pattern of communication. Only when the outcomes of the assessment are clear can effective alternative and augmentative communication approaches be put into place. These are crucial if we are to empower the child with SLD/PMLD as a competent communicator – by whatever means!

There are a range of alternative approaches to communication nowadays, which offer meaningful and enriching experiences to children with severe communication impairments. These may be through objects of reference, or Information Technology (Detheridge

1997), through signing or symbol systems or assistive technology embracing a variety of speech synthesisers and switch control devices. Any of these means can unlock the door to communication, which in the past may have been so firmly shut for this group of pupils.

Goldbart (1994) reminds us that "it is by being treated as communicators that we become communicators" (p. 16). In the past, children with SLD/PMLD who did not communicate through conventional means (e.g. speech, signs, etc.) were seen as non-communicators. Is this true today? Is it more that our inability, as their teachers or therapists, to identify accurately their idiosyncratic modes of communication prevents us from enabling them to become communicators?

Communication is an intrinsic element of our basic humanity. Our children with SLD/PMLD are entitled to their status as human beings. Without it, respect and dignity are often denied. Our task is therefore one of identifying, with them and their parents/carers, the most effective means of communication for them, and ensuring that all potential communication partners are aware of this.

Assessing Communication offers practitioners a tangible, logical and incisive means of doing just this. Its penetrating analysis of communicative competence displays instantly its relevance as an assessment tool for children with SLD/PMLD. It acknowledges the centrality of communication in the curriculum, and that the setting offering maximum opportunities for communication assessment in a learning context is the classroom. The design of the materials is skilful, and enables the classroom practitioner, over time, to construct a profile of a child's communication skills. The link between assessment, teaching, monitoring and evaluation are strong, facilitating a cyclical process of communication development that keeps the child in focus throughout. This book will be welcomed and acclaimed for the practical approach it adopts, and the reflective insights it generates.

Barry Carpenter
Centre for the Study of Special Education
Westminster College
Oxford

References

Detheridge, T. (1997) Bridging the communication gap (for pupils with profound and multiple learning difficulties), *British Journal of Special Education* **24**(1), 21–6.

Fitton, P. (1994) *Listen to Me: Communicating the Needs of People with Profound Intellectual and Multiple Disabilities*, London: Jessica Kingsley.

Goldbart, J. (1994) "Opening the communication curriculum to students with PMLDs" in J. Ware (ed.) *Educating Children with Profound and Multiple Learning Difficulties*, London: David Fulton.

Acknowledgements

We would like to thank the staff, pupils and parents of The Redway School (until 1993 Queens School) in Milton Keynes for their support and tolerance during the development of the Communication Assessment.

Particular thanks are due to Richard Fraser (The Redway School) and Peter Skingley (Queens School), who enabled us to develop our ideas and complete the work.

Mavis Allwood of Haversham First School, Milton Keynes, also contributed her ideas to Assessment Band Four.

We remain indebted to every pupil at The Redway School who continue to teach us the value and fun of effective communication.

Introduction

The Redway School Communication Assessment is designed to assess the early communicative development of pupils with severe learning difficulties (SLD) and profound and multiple learning difficulties (PMLD). The development work took place at The Redway School in Milton Keynes. This introduction will discuss the theoretical background to the assessment, demonstrate the link to curriculum development and explain the assessment format.

The assessment is based on the functional (or sociolinguistic) theory of language acquisition with some reference to the semantic theory. The fundamental principle underlining the functional theory is the use of language to communicate and to affect the behaviour of others. The context in which communication takes place affects the speaker's meaning.

Jerome Bruner is generally considered to be the main protagonist of this theory. He emphasises the need for a partner in the development of functional communication, where the role of the adult is to interact with the child and to help make the speech intentions clear (Bruner 1975).

> Early language acquisition . . . depends heavily on the use of context by both mother and child in forming and interpreting messages. Successful early communication requires a shared and familiar context to aid the partners in making their communicative intentions clear to each other. (Bruner 1983: 128)

Bruner also identifies the social processes that begin in the earliest pre-verbal games and continue through advanced language development. These key activities are turn-taking and role interchange. More or different functions are acquired as the child matures. The content of the utterance is linked to the meaning that the child intends to express.

Theoretical background

The theory of speech acts is a further development in the functional theory of language acquisition. The basis of this theory is that an utterance cannot be analysed out of context. It is the intention of the speaker combined with the understanding of the listener that gives the utterance meaning. The first meaningful words are those that link to pre-verbal acts already established (Harris 1990).

The Redway School Communication Assessment also embraces a semantic approach. This is concerned with the meaning of language. Children's first words express an understanding about their environment; the meaning is specific to context but may be understood by a familiar person. The emphasis in a semantic theory of language acquisition is on receptive language. Children are seen as able to express only those meanings of objects and events that they have understood. Language is therefore interwoven with cognitive development.

Play

This brief background is not intended to be a complete discussion of all aspects of play, but to emphasise the important role of play in the development of communication.

For older students, much of this play can take place in creative activities such as drama roleplays. Whatever the level of play, children's favoured activities form the ideal shared activities that will be more likely to motivate them towards better and more successful communication.

Athey (1984) commented: "Language and play have been found to be mutually reinforcing". This is one reason why the authors decided to include play in the Redway School Communication Assessment. The authors follow John and Elizabeth Newson's description of play as a "Partly random and infinitely flexible opportunity for the extension of, and re-orientation of, the mind and spirit" (Newson & Newson 1979: 11).

The earliest form of play is the discovery of pleasure in exploratory movement and social activity (Ellis 1973). Here the child repeats random movements or vocalisations which give pleasure.

Social play, or people play as it can be referred to (Gerard 1986), begins when adults respond to the child's behaviours. The child enjoys the attention and tries strategies to repeat the experience. This leads to the earliest turn-taking, when the adult copies the child's behaviour and the child repeats it. These early games may also involve hiding, such as "peep bo", which develops awareness of object permanence.

Play with objects is at first exploratory – mouthing, hitting, banging, etc. At this stage the child can relate to an object or to an adult, but not both. Later the child learns to share experiences with an adult, such as playing with a toy together, taking turns to hit a drum or watching an event together. Here the child is relating to both toy or event and adult. The pleasure of a shared experience helps develop the social aspects of communication. Symbolic play skills begin to emerge when the child uses real objects imaginatively, as in pretending to drink from a cup, or talking into a telephone. The next stage is the involvement of the adult in this play.

The link between language and cognition is much discussed. Marianne Lowe's work revealed that symbolic play coincides with the emergence of language, especially the aspect of language linked to putting words together. Lowe (1975) and Westby (1980) developed the idea that symbolic (play) skills were essential prerequisites for meaningful communication.

More recent studies have successfully demonstrated that teaching cognition can enable children to develop appropriate language skills (Harrison *et al.* 1987). Imaginative play continues to be a key area for language development. Children begin to act out familiar events, clarifying activities and sequences in their minds. This play also allows for endless repetitions of the language used for the chosen event, such as shops, cafés and so on. More imaginative play involving less familiar events develops as the child matures.

All other forms of play give the child the opportunity to use and develop communication skills, whether with peers or adults. For example, construction activity involves planning while physical play allows the child to experience the meaning of action words.

As children mature, co-operative play with peers allows them to use a variety of language skills such as negotiating, explaining, planning and directing.

Humour

Humour has been observed with interest at The Redway School. Its links with play have led the authors to include it in the assessment. While there are several theories of humour, the authors have chosen the cognitive theory that describes the child's growing understanding of incongruity as the essence of humour (McGhee 1979). This begins during the second year of life and is closely linked to imaginative play. McGhee describes definite stages in the development of humour as follows.

Stage 1
This is the incongruous match of image, object and action. The child will pretend that an object is something else by acting upon it with the intention of making others laugh.

Stage 2
This overlaps with the first but essentially it is now a verbal statement that demonstrates the incongruity, an example being the giving of names to objects and people which the child knows to be incorrect.

Stage 3
The child now has greater conceptual understanding and finds incongruity in gender changes, pictures that look wrong (e.g. a bicycle with square wheels), repetitious rhyming words and nonsense words.

Stage 4
The child now begins to understand verbal puns and double meanings. Cognitively the child is now able to keep two ideas in mind at the same time and thus see both the serious and the incongruous.

Communication curriculum development

In the late 1980s and early 1990s schools for children with severe learning difficulties began to develop communication curricula that moved from the structural approach of language development to a functional approach (Coupe & Goldbart 1988). The process and meaning of communication became more important than the learning of sentence structure or vocabulary (Latham & Miles 1993).

At The Redway School the authors began changing the language curriculum in 1992, establishing a communication policy which recognised communication as central to the school's whole curriculum. Teaching communication skills was not confined to timetabled sessions alone, but fully integrated into the life of the school. It was recognised that all staff are involved in the teaching of communication skills. As such, in-service training would be needed at intervals to enable staff to communicate through signs, symbols, or other augmentative and alternative systems. In addition an active partnership with parents and carers was encouraged to provide a total communication system for each pupil. A communication curriculum was devised to be followed by all staff to ensure that each teacher would build on the work done by the previous teacher and therefore provide continuity and progression.

The communication curriculum framework involves certain fundamental principles. The use of language is defined as a means to communicate and to affect the behaviour of others. Success is judged by effectiveness in conveying the speaker's meaning. The main aim is more effective communication. Functional communication covers all aspects of development from the earliest pre-intentional behaviours through to more sophisticated use. It has a special application for older pupils with severe learning difficulties, concentrating on developing communication for everyday living.

The communication curriculum falls naturally into four bands which are described as follows.

Band One – pre-verbal

This is subdivided into pre-intentional and intentional communication. At the earliest stages pupils respond only with reflexes to internal stimuli, for instance crying with hunger or pain. This develops into responding to external stimuli such as pleasant or unpleasant events in the environment. The pupil does not intend to communicate, but the adult learns to interpret the behaviours and act upon them, for example, feeding a hungry child.

Still without intending to communicate, the pupil begins to try to act upon the environment. A typical behaviour would be reaching for a drink. Once again the adult interprets the behaviour and responds to it. As pupils become intentional communicators, they act purposefully on adults and objects with the intention of communicating, for example by looking at the bottle and then at the adult, communicating clearly that they want the bottle.

This intentional behaviour develops until the pupil has several meanings that can be conveyed using body language, facial expression or vocalisation.

Band Two – first meanings

This band covers the development of the first words from the time that pupils have something definite to communicate until they have a word, sign or symbol vocabulary of about 50 words.

It is called first meanings because the first communications are not clear words, but ideas or meanings which pupils wish to communicate. An example would be indicating a desire for more dinner by looking longingly at the serving dish and then gesturing to the server.

First meanings are usually communicated initially through facial expression and body language, then gesture and vocalisation, and finally, with a clear sign or word. However, pupils are very individual about how they communicate at this level and in what they choose to say.

Different authors identify a variety of first meanings; however, Coupe *et al.* (1988b) compiled a list of ten for pupils with severe learning difficulties.

Band Three – words, signs and symbols

At this band pupils are beginning to link words (signs or symbols) into simple sentences and phrases. Pupils must begin to use whatever language system they have for different functions such as socialising, communicating information, initiating conversation, making requests, describing, directing, questioning and repairing misunderstandings.

Basic conversational skill becomes important. As pupils begin to use longer sentences for more purposes, articulation problems may become more obvious and inhibit the communication.

Other pupils may demonstrate a good understanding of language but have problems expressing themselves clearly. Alternative and augmentative methods of communication may have been introduced during the first meanings band, but should now become an essential part of the pupil's total communication system.

Band Four – expanding communication skill

This band is for pupils with good basic language skills. They will be linking their ideas into complex sentences and be ready for a wider range of activities in the English curriculum. The emphasis is still on language use, but on using language for more difficult functions such as reasoning, predicting and planning. Additional emphasis is placed on developing better conversational skills.

As vocabularies and skills increase, pupils can spend more time on the creative use of language – telling stories, poems and taking part in drama. Life skills are introduced; these include use of the telephone, social sight reading activities, handling money and time skills.

Aims of the assessment

Addressing the functional communication skills of all the pupils in a school for children with severe learning difficulties led the authors to look at several published assessments. For example, *Affective Communication Assessment* (Coupe *et al.* 1988a), *Pre-Verbal Communication Schedule* (Kiernan & Reid 1987), *Derbyshire Language Scheme* (Knowles & Masidlover 1982) and others are extremely useful and used within the school, but it was felt that further assessment was needed to produce a cohesive picture (see also p. 74).

The reasons for this are to
- allow for observation and recording of pupils' individual ways of communicating, enabling us to construct a total communication system for each pupil
- focus our attention on our own communication styles, making them more appropriate and consistent from all adults
- focus our attention on the ability of pupils to control or affect their environment through communication
- acknowledge development across a range of language skills so that teacher, therapist and parent views would be harnessed together
- ensure continuity across the school with each teacher building on the work of the previous one
- look at the overall development of the pupils, relating communication skills to cognitive ability
- meet all the needs of our pupils from the earliest communicative level through to pupils working within the National Curriculum English Level 1, and include social communication skills development.

Communication assessment framework

Successful functional communication at all levels depends on opportunities to:	Functional communication	Communication systems available	Developmental language level
	BAND ONE *Pre-intentional*		0–9 months
Make choices	Likes	Cry	
	Dislikes	Still	
	Wants	Excited movement	
	Rejects	Watchful	
	Distinguishes between familiar and unfamiliar	Vocalise Facial expression Reach Extended reach	
Share activities	*Intentional* Draws attention to self	Point Body language	
	Requests	Look	
	Greets	Gesture	
	Protests and rejects	Protowords	
	Gives information		
Take time to respond	Responds		
	BAND TWO Existence	Signs	9–18 months
	Disappearance	Words	
	Recurrence	Speech output devices	
	Possession		
	Rejection		
	Non-existence		
Initiate communication	Location		
	Action		
	Agent		
	Object		
	Attributes		
	BAND THREE Socialisation	Symbols	18 months–3 years
Give directions	Requests	2–3 word utterances, not always intelligible	
	Gives information		
	Describes	May combine several methods of communication in the same phrase	
	Directs		
	Questions		
	Repairs misunderstandings		
	BAND FOUR Gives and shares information	Expanding vocabulary More complex sentences	3–5 years
Repair misunderstandings	Describes		
	Directs	Conversation skills	
	Questions	Using language for learning	
	Reasons and predicts		
	Plans and evaluates		
	Negotiates		
	Conversation skills		
	Expresses feelings		
	CREATIVE USE OF LANGUAGE LIFE SKILLS		

Use of the assessment format

How to place a pupil within a band

The assessment begins by selecting the appropriate assessment band. The following points are intended to help the assessor decide. Some pupils bridge two of the bands while others are more difficult to place. It has been our experience that once use of the band has commenced, it soon becomes clear if the use of a band is pitched either too low or too high. The assessor should
- read through the description of the bands
- observe the child communicating in a variety of settings
- take careful note of the meanings being conveyed
- take careful note of spontaneous communications
- take note of the adult's level of communications
- talk to those who know the child well – parents, support staff and others.

Having decided on a band of communicative ability, refer to the appropriate part of this book for further guidance on how to complete the assessment.

The bands follow on from one another with areas of skill developing through all four. The assessment bands are designed to be used by the class teacher in conjunction with the parents and support staff. The heading of each section and comments made by the assessor are then used to describe communicative competence in the English section of the Annual Review Report.

Future planning

Any assessment must lead the assessor to know where to help. Helping pupils to communicate effectively involves
- examining adults' communications
- creating situations that are conducive to communication
- learning to allow pupils the opportunity to control the adult safely and enjoyably.

The bands have specific headings to guide the assessor in future planning.

Further advice required

In all four bands, it is recognised that many pupils with severe learning difficulties may have other problems. Hearing impairment, visual impairments, physical handicaps or medical conditions will affect communicative ability. Further advice in these, or other areas, may need to be sought.

Approach to communication

In Bands One and Two, it is recognised that these pupils often need to be approached in a certain way if successful communication is to be made. For example, it is often necessary to join pupils in an activity of their choosing, and allow them to lead the interaction.

Maintaining current level of communication

In all four bands, enjoyable activities are identified where communication is possible and easiest to establish. It is also recognised that for some pupils progress may not be possible, thus creating situations to maintain appropriate communication is vital.

Teaching style

Here are some matters that should be considered in all four bands:
- appropriate level of language used by the adult
- use of facial expression, natural gesture or pointing by the adult
- using objects of reference, sign language, symbol books/timetables as an aid to understanding language
- allowing the pupil to initiate communication
- carefully considered use of questioning
- offering comments on pupils' actions
- modelling the next stage of a pupil's communication development
- lesson planning to include appropriate opportunities for communication.

Goals and activities to advance communication

For many pupils it will be important to select certain goals. These will be highlighted in all four assessment bands. For example at Band Three a pupil may be requesting, describing and giving information, but not directing; directing may then become a specific goal implemented through the role reversal in some curriculum areas.

Use of alternative and augmentative communication (AAC)

Pupils use different forms of AAC in varying ways. Which methods are to be used, and those who will take responsibility for producing and maintaining them, should be entered in this section, when pupils are in Bands Three and Four.

Intelligibility

This is an area of great difficulty for many youngsters with severe learning difficulties. It is also an area that may be difficult to improve. Advice should be sought from a speech and language therapist to see if anything can be done, when pupils are in Bands Three and Four.

Communication Assessment Band One

Pre-Verbal

Band One looks at the earliest (pre-verbal) communications that pupils make. It is subdivided into pre-intentional and intentional communication.

At the earliest pre-intentional level, pupils respond with reflexes to internal stimuli, for instance crying with hunger or pain. This develops into responding to external stimuli such as pleasant or unpleasant events in the environment. The pupil does not intend to communicate, but the adult interprets the behaviours and acts upon them, for example feeding a hungry child.

Still without intending to communicate, the pupil begins to act upon the environment. A typical behaviour would be reaching for a drink. Once again the adult interprets the behaviour and responds to it. As pupils become intentional communicators, they act purposefully on adults and objects with the intention of communicating, for example by looking at their bottle and then at the adult, communicating clearly that they want more drink.

This intentional communication develops until pupils have several meanings they can communicate using body language, facial expression and vocalisation.

Looking at the pre-verbal communications assessed in Band One requires close observation and discussion with those who know the pupil best. The following is a guide to gathering the appropriate information to complete the assessment.

Observations

- Observe the pupils interacting with someone who knows them well, for example parents, carers or support staff.
- Discuss the adults' interpretation of the pupils' behaviours.
- Observe the pupil interacting with a variety of sensory stimuli. To guide your observation, the *Affective Communication Assessment* (Coupe *et al.* 1988a) may be helpful.

- Observe the pupils interacting with a variety of objects; for example do they just look intently at the object or do they act upon it?
- Observe the pupils interacting with familiar and unfamiliar people, situations and objects. Do they distinguish between the two?
- Observe the pupils in situations where it is possible for them to show the negative behaviours of disliking and rejecting.

Note that play and comprehension apply to both pre-intentional and intentional communicators. The assessments can be found on p. 15.

Record-keeping

Keep an accurate record of the pupil's own idiosyncratic ways of communicating to help others who do not know the pupil so well. In all four bands examples are given of some of the methods the pupil may be using to convey different meanings, but in the authors' opinion, careful recording of what the pupil is actually doing is essential. The following is offered as a guide to record-keeping.

- The *Affective Communication Assessment* (Coupe *et al.* 1988a) can be helpful and provides a record-keeping form which looks at the small and varied ways a pupil is communicating.
- Having recorded an observation, it is helpful to allow others to record their observations so that agreement can be reached.
- At these early levels of communicative ability it is important to record not only how the pupil conveyed something but also your interpretation and the general context in which it occurred.
- Having recorded your observations, it becomes easier to complete the band accurately and comprehensively.

Liaison with parents, carers and other staff

The pupil's communication exists and develops with many people, and in many different situations. Liaison is essential. The following are offered as suggestions to help.

- A questionnaire can be sent out prior to any discussion.
- Allow support staff some time to observe and record interaction.
- Allow time for as many people as possible to complete the band together.
- If some key people are unable to join the discussion, being sent a questionnaire will enable them to contribute by phone or by returning the questionnaire.

The pre-verbal meanings being conveyed at this level are taken from Coupe *et al.* (1988a).

Hearing, vision, physical difficulties, medical and other problems

Note should be made of significant problems.

Likes (0.1)

The different ways that the pupils show that they like a person, activity or action should be recorded here, e.g. stilling to an activity or object of interest.

Dislikes (0.2)

The pupils' ability to communicate negative as well as positive meanings is important. Note should be made of how the pupils show dislike of a person, activity or action, e.g. physically withdrawing from an activity or object.

Wants (0.3)

Note should be made of the different ways that pupils use to show they want a person, activity or action, e.g. general body excitement on presentation of their bottle.

Rejects (0.4)

This is another important negative communication. It is often similar to the behaviour accompanying dislike but is usually stronger and more persistent. Note should be made how the pupils show rejection of a person, activity or action.

Distinguishes between familiar and unfamiliar (0.5)

This is an important observation and affects future plans. Note should be made of the different methods that pupils use to show they distinguish between familiar and unfamiliar objects, actions, activities or people.

Makes eye contact (0.6)

Eye contact is essential for successful communication. The level of competence that pupils show in making and sustaining eye contact and the length of time this can be maintained should be entered in this box.

Guide to Assessment Band One: pre-intentional communication

Examples from Band One

Wants (a person, activity or action) (0.3)

> *Lizzie continues to communicate her wants by reaching out with her left hand, general body excitement, or staring at objects that are out of reach. Over the year she has started to show an ability to reach and sometimes look to the adult to communicate "wanting". This intentional behaviour is not yet established, but very pleasing.*

EXAMPLES: BY CRYING   BY SHOWING BODY EXCITEMENT
BY REACHING   BY EXTENDED REACH

Rejects (a person, activity or action) (0.4)

> *Lizzie is more definite in her rejection. She will show annoyance vocally and facially if provoked. Lizzie will also push objects off her tray if she does not want them.*

EXAMPLES: BY CRYING   BY TURNING AWAY
BY BREAKING EYE CONTACT   BY PUSHING AWAY

Distinguishes between familiar and unfamiliar (0.5)

> *Lizzie has always distinguished key familiar people and objects since her entry into school. However, this familiarity has now diversified, so she will distinguish particular music, sensory activities and carers. She shows this by clear smiling, happy vocalisations and general body excitement.*

EXAMPLES: BY SPECIFIC EXCITEMENT AT SIGHT OF PARENT OR FAVOURED TOY, e.g. BOTTLE, ETC.
BY SEEKING COMFORT FROM FAMILIAR CARE GIVER

Turn-taking (0.7)

The ability to take turns in reciprocal interaction is also essential for successful communication. At this stage it is usually possible only with the adult following the pupil's action and the pupil then continuing it. The ability to take turns and sustain turn-taking should be entered in this box; for example the adult pats a table top after the pupil and the pupil repeats the action to sustain it.

Play (0.8)

Play is vital to communication. The earliest form of play is enjoying body movement. As play develops, it involves play with people or object play. It is not until the pupil becomes an intentional communicator that the object and people play become integrated. Notes should be made of the different ways that pupils enjoy play and the type of play preferred.

Comprehension (0.9)

At the beginning of early communication development, pupils do not follow words as such. However, they do react to tone of voice, make sense of familiar routines and at the end of this stage begin to follow the odd key word in a familiar routine. Notes should be made of the different situations and tones of voice or key words to which the pupils respond.

Pupils are said to communicate intentionally when they are able to indicate that they want an object or action. This usually involves looking towards the object or the source of the action and back towards the adult to ensure that the adult has got the message, e.g. looking at the mug that the adult is drinking from and back at the adult to convey that the pupil would also like a drink. The message is clearly understood by the adult as are other early intentional communications.

Guide to Assessment Band One: intentional communication

Draws attention to self, events, objects or people (1.1)

Pupils begin to show this early communication by vocalising and looking at a person to communicate that they want some attention. They may vocalise and look at an object and back to the adult to draw the adult's attention to it.

Requests objects, actions, information or recurrence of actions (1.2)

At this stage pupils use an adult as a means of requesting, for example putting the adult's hand on the door knob as a request to open the door. The different ways that pupils request objects, actions or recurrence of actions should be entered in this section.

Greeting (1.3)

The pupils are beginning to recognise the social possibility of communication. The early greetings are now observed, for example pupils holds out their hands and vocalise to greet familiar people as they enter the room.

Protests and rejects (1.4)

The pupils are now able to communicate clearly that they will not tolerate an object or action, for example stiffening as the adult puts on a coat, making it difficult for the adult to complete the action.

Gives information (1.5)

As the ability to communicate develops, so the pupils explore a widening range of meanings that they can communicate. Giving simple information is now developed, for example by pointing and showing the adult a new pair of shoes.

Responds leading to yes/no response (1.6)

The pupils' responses become more defined. The smile to show "like" may become a vocalisation and head nod to communicate "yes". Comment on the methods that the pupils use to communicate "yes" and "no".

Play (1.7)

As the pupils become intentional in their communication, so people and object play become integrated, for example the pupil shakes a bell and gives it to the adult gesturing for the adult to shake.

Verbal comprehension (1.8)

As the pupil becomes more actively communicative, he begins to respond to spoken words and phrases in some contexts. It is important to note the situations in which the pupil understands spoken language as well as the actual phrases.

Guide to future planning

Once the information has been gathered and sorted into the appropriate boxes the assessor is ready to make future plans. To help guide the assessor's ideas, this area of Band One is divided into five sections.

Further advice required (A)

This is the place to note that understanding of the pupil's communication is incomplete and help is needed from other professionals.

Approach to communication (B)

All pupils are individuals and will respond more positively to a particular approach. Consider visual problems and the best direction of approach. In what position can the pupil see the adult's face and how closely should the adult be positioned? Seating, lighting and other environmental factors may need to be taken into account. Does the adult need to touch the pupil first to gain attention? If pupils are sensitive to touch, it may be better to say their name. How can adults show the pupils they are listening to them?

Teaching style (C)

Both from the assessor's observations and from personal knowledge of the pupil's level of communication, it will be clear if the adult needs to adapt the style of communication to ensure successful interaction. The following points should be considered:
- Interaction must be motivating and enjoyable. Search out those things the pupil enjoys and use them for communication.
- Learning negative communication is as important as learning positive communication. Decide on strategies for respecting and responding to all the disliking and rejecting behaviours exhibited by the pupil.
- Understanding of events and communication are very limited at this level. Comprehension can be aided by the use of objects of reference to indicate what is about to happen. The adult's body language and tone of voice are more important than the actual words. Ensuring the pupil has a familiar carer can lessen distress and confusion caused by changes.

Maintaining current level of communication (D)

In our experience it is important to note the activities that can be used to maintain current levels of communicative competence. For some pupils it is unrealistic to set new goals but working to maintain inter-action is appropriate. For such pupils, this goal can be stated on their individual educational programme.

Consider the following points:
- activities that the pupil enjoys (including most receptive time of day and other environmental factors)
- routines during which the pupil makes a response.

Goals and activities to advance communication (E)

When filling in the boxes, the assessor may have identified areas where current skills could be developed further, e.g. reaching for a bottle on a shelf could be encouraged to be more intentional if the pupil is encouraged to look back at the adult as it is given. This may be facilitated by bringing the bottle to the adult's face before handing it to the pupil. Gaps in the assessment may become apparent, e.g. limited eye contact. The filling of these gaps may be appropriate goals to set.

Hearing

Band One:
the assessment

Pupil's name:

Date:

Vision

Physical difficulties

Medical and other problems

First stage: pre-intentional communicator

There are two main stages of development: investigations into the pupils' communication will indicate whether they are pre-intentional or intentional communicators.

Comment on the behaviours the pupil uses which convey the following.

Likes (a person, activity or action) (0.1)

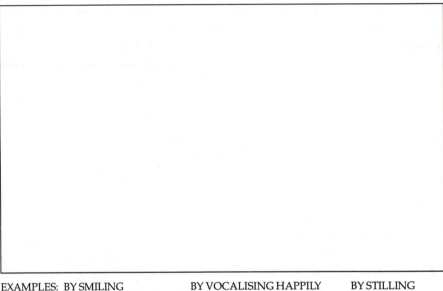

EXAMPLES: BY SMILING   BY VOCALISING HAPPILY   BY STILLING
          BY BODY GESTURE   BY FACIAL EXPRESSION

Dislikes (a person, activity or action) (0.2)

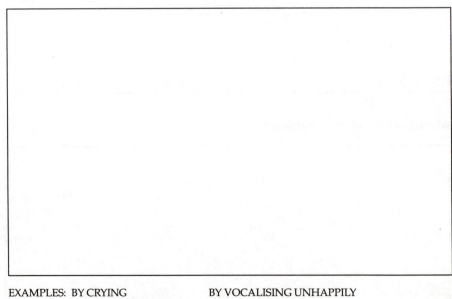

EXAMPLES: BY CRYING   BY VOCALISING UNHAPPILY
          BY LOOKING AWAY   BY PUSHING AWAY
          BY FACIAL EXPRESSION BY BODY MOVEMENT

Wants (a person, activity or action) (0.3)

EXAMPLES: BY CRYING   BY SHOWING BODY EXCITEMENT
               BY REACHING   BY EXTENDED REACH

Rejects (a person, activity or action) (0.4)

EXAMPLES: BY CRYING   BY TURNING AWAY
               BY BREAKING EYE CONTACT   BY PUSHING AWAY

Distinguishes between familiar and unfamiliar (0.5)

EXAMPLES: BY SPECIFIC EXCITEMENT AT SIGHT OF PARENT OR FAVOURED TOY, e.g.
               BOTTLE, ETC.
               BY SEEKING COMFORT FROM FAMILIAR CARE GIVER

Makes eye contact (0.6)

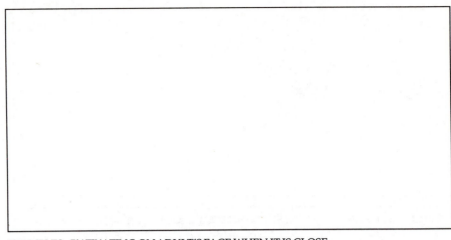

EXAMPLES: BY FIXATING ON ADULT'S FACE WHEN IT IS CLOSE
BY FIXATING ON AN OFFERED TOY
BY SHARING ATTENTION WITH TOY AND ADULT

Turn-taking (0.7)

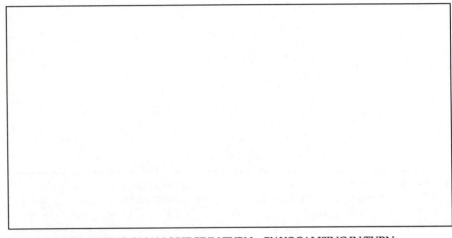

EXAMPLES: BY ACTING ON AN OBJECT IN TURN   BY VOCALISING IN TURN
BY TAKING PART IN PHYSICAL PLAY ROUTINES

Notes

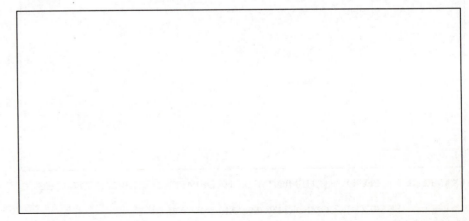

Second stage: intentional communicator

At this stage the pupil behaves purposefully in order to communicate. Now comment on the ways the pupil does the following.

Draws attention to self, events, objects or people (1.1)

EXAMPLES: BY VOCALISING AND LOOKING   BY TUGGING AND PULLING
BY COMING CLOSE AND LEANING

Requests objects, actions, information or recurrence of actions (1.2)

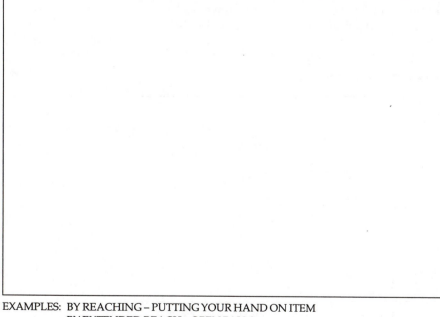

EXAMPLES: BY REACHING – PUTTING YOUR HAND ON ITEM
BY EXTENDED REACH – OPEN PALM
BY GESTURES (ARMS UP CARRY)

Greeting (1.3)

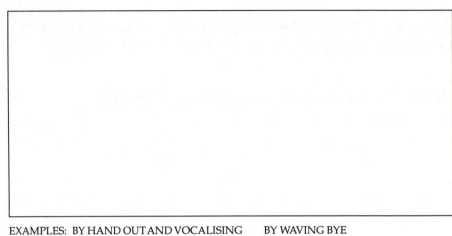

EXAMPLES: BY HAND OUT AND VOCALISING   BY WAVING BYE
BY COMING AND HUGGING

Protests and rejects (1.4)

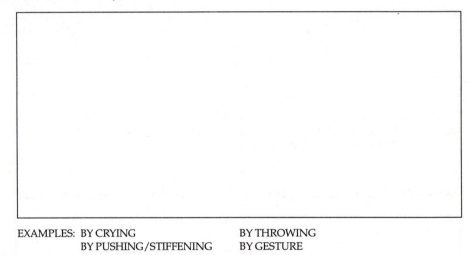

EXAMPLES: BY CRYING   BY THROWING
BY PUSHING/STIFFENING   BY GESTURE

Gives information (1.5)

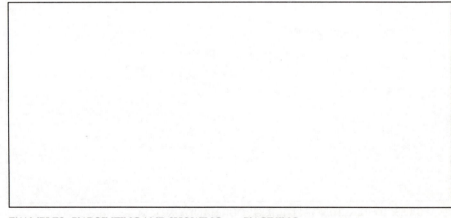

EXAMPLES: BY POINTING AND SHOWING   BY GIVING
BY TAKING YOU TO SHOW WHAT HAS HAPPENED

Responds leading to yes/no response (1.6)

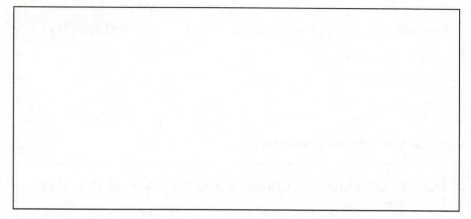

EXAMPLES: BY VOCALISING – HEAD NOD "YES"   BY GESTURE
                  BY HEAD SHAKE – "NO"

Play (0.8/1.7)

Comprehension (0.9/1.8)

Future planning

Further advice required (A)

> Hearing, visual, occupational therapy, etc. (circle and specify).

Approach to communication (B)

> Describe the situation, positioning and approach which enable best interaction.

Teaching style (C)

> Describe level of language, use of eye contact, use of objects of reference, etc.

Maintaining current level of communication (D)

Goals and activities to advance communication (E)

First Meanings

Band Two covers the development of the first words from the time that pupils have something definite to communicate, until they have a word, sign or symbol vocabulary of about 50 words.

Introduction

It is called first meanings because the first communications, rather than being clear words, are ideas or meanings that the pupil wishes to communicate. An example would be to indicate a desire for more dinner by looking longingly at the serving dish and then gesturing to the server.

First meanings are usually communicated initially through facial expression and body language, then gesture and vocalisation, and finally with a clear word or sign. However, most pupils are very individual about how they communicate at this level and in what they choose to say.

It is worth noting that one behaviour (gesture, vocalisation, etc.) can have various meanings. For example, a wave can mean "Goodbye", " Go away", or "I don't want to".

Different authors identify a variety of first meanings. Coupe *et al.* (1988b) compiled a list of ten for specific application for pupils with severe learning difficulties. It is these which are used in the Redway School Communication Assessment. Gerard (1986) describes more meanings. For pupils who remain at this level for a long time, her additional assessment may be helpful.

Many pupils, once they express a large number of these meanings, develop their system into the one and two word levels of expressive language described in other assessments.

Band Two is for those pupils who are able to convey most of the meanings listed as intentional communication. In addition Coupe *et al.* (1988b) suggest that the pupil should be able to achieve the following cognitive skills:

Prerequisites for the use of Band Two

- means for obtaining desired environmental events
- visual permanence and pursuit of objects
- object related schemes.

19

Pupils with severe physical handicaps may develop some of these cognitive skills through use of switches and microtechnology.

The pupil should be able to show clear positive and negative responses. These may be idiosyncratic and recognisable only by close family, but if they are consistent then they should be documented.

The pupil should be able to relate to both adult and object, e.g. give joint attention to situations and objects. This means that the pupil is no longer fixed on one thing but can play with an adult and an object.

The pupil should be developing a means of pointing, e.g. by fist, hand or eye.

The pupil's methods of conveying information are becoming more stylised, probably using a specific gesture to communicate. An early example is waving "bye" to people and objects to send them away.

Looking at the communications assessed in Band Two requires close observation and discussion with those who know the pupil. The following is a guide to gathering appropriate information to complete the assessment.

Gathering information

Observations

The assessor should watch the pupil in different situations.

- A busy classroom is not the best place to observe pupils at this level communicating to the best of their ability (as most interactions will be idiosyncratic and directed at one person). However, it will show pupils' level of play and how successful they are at gaining attention and interacting with others.
- Time should be allowed for the pupil to play with an adult to demonstrate the highest levels of communication the pupil can achieve. Using a favourite activity and being an attentive listener will encourage the pupil to express a range of meanings.
- As the pupil begins to convey a few of the meanings outlined, it may be necessary to set up situations to encourage the use of other meanings, or to see if they are present. This is always a satisfying activity for parent and teachers as the pupil can suddenly appear a more competent communicator.
- Observation at mealtimes will give lots of useful information, including how the pupils ask for more, indicate that they would like a drink and show when they have had enough.

Record-keeping

It is suggested that a record is kept of communications as they occur throughout the year. The pupil's activities and adult's interpretations should be noted.

Liaison with parents, carers and other staff

The pupil's communication exists and develops with many people, and in many different situations. As such, liaison is essential. The following are offered as helpful suggestions.
- A questionnaire can be sent out prior to any discussion.
- Support staff could be allowed some time to observe and record interaction.
- Time could be allowed for as many people as is possible to sit down and complete the assessment together.
- If some key people were unable to join the discussion, being sent a questionnaire would enable them to contribute by phone or by returning the completed questionnaire.

Reference should be made to these guidelines before completing Band Two.

Guide to Assessment Band Two

Hearing, vision, physical difficulties, medical and other problems

Significant problems should be noted.

Verbal comprehension (2.1)

As pupils enter this level they recognise key words in routine situations, often referred to as "situational understanding", for example, "home" is understood at home time, "drink" is understood at drinks time. Slowly the understanding of routine words and phrases grows. Ensuring that staff use similar vocabulary can help build up comprehension at this level. This means always relating the words to the concrete object, person or action.

Play/(or for a much older person) "favoured activity" (2.2)

This is an important section of the assessment, giving information about the pupil's level of cognitive development, and helping with future planning. Notes should be made as to whether the pupil plays in the following ways:
- The pupil is physically exploring or visually examining objects and materials.
- The pupil is acting upon objects by pushing, banging, throwing, exploring, etc.
- The pupil is playing with two objects together such as banging two toys together.
- During play, the pupil refers to the adult for approval or turn-taking, thus indicating an ability to refer to a person and object.

- The pupil is at the earliest stages of imaginative play, pretending to drink from a cup or talking into the telephone.
- The pupil gives drinks to an adult or dolly or takes part in similar single sequence play.

Guide to meanings communicated

Existence (2.3)

The intention is for the pupils to show the adult the object, sharing their knowledge of the existence of the object. An example may be pointing out an aeroplane flying over. This gesture may lead towards the use of the word "look", or naming of objects.

Disappearance (2.4)

Pupils' knowledge of object permanence is demonstrated by their comments when objects or people go away. Pupils may turn up their hands and shrug when they drop their pencil and lose it. Pupils at this level may enjoy hiding or "peep bo" games. This may lead towards the use of the words "gone", "no", or "bye".

Recurrence (2.5)

The requesting demonstrated in Band One develops into a request for more of an item, action or person. Pupils may indicate a desire for more pushes on a swing or for a repetition of a favourite song. This leads towards the word or sign "more", "again", or "want".

Possession (2.6)

The pupils begin to express a relationship between an object, person or activity and themselves For example, when pupils see a biscuit they point to themselves (especially when asked "Who would like a biscuit?"). This is described as possession. Pupils also begin to claim ownership of possessions and people, e.g. "mine".

Rejection (2.7)

The pupils clearly reject an object, action, event or person. This is a continuation of the functional language (dislikes) described in Band One. Pupils should be encouraged to use more formal systems of rejection, for instance saying or signing "no".

Recurrence (requests an item to be returned or repetition of an action) (2.5)

> *Carl currently repeats an action or reaches for more of something. The generalised label (sign of "more") has been used once but is not established.*

EXAMPLES: BY LOOKING – TO ADULT AND VOCALISING
BY GESTURE – REPEATING PART OF THE ACTION
BY POINTING – POINTS TO OBJECT TO GET IT BACK
BY WORD, SIGN OR SYMBOL FOR OBJECT – "MORE", "WANT", "AGAIN"

Possession (indicates relationship between an object, person or activity to self) (2.6)

> *Carl points to himself and says "me" to indicate that something is his.*
>
> *He is beginning to say "arl" for "Carl" to indicate possession.*

EXAMPLES: BY POINTING TO SELF WHEN ASKED "WHOSE TOY IS THIS?"
BY WORD, SIGN OR SYMBOL – "MINE", "MY GO", "ME"

Rejection (clearly rejects an object, action, event or person) (2.7)

> *Carl looks away, stands firm, "blanks off", walks away or ignores to reject. He does not yet use the more generalised communication of shaking his head.*

EXAMPLES: BY PUSHING AWAY PERSON   BY SHAKING HEAD
BY WORD, SIGN OR SYMBOL – "GO", "NO", "GO AWAY"

Non-existence (2.8)

Non-existence is demonstrated when something is not where the pupil expected to find it. For example, when asked to fetch a coat, the pupil comes back looking puzzled and shrugging shoulders because it is not on the peg. As with "rejection" and "disappearance", this meaning may be communicated by the word "gone".

Location (2.9)

The pupils convey the position of an object or the position in which they would like an object to be placed. This may be indicated by pointing, leading to the word "there".

Action (2.10)

The requesting messages from Band One begin to clarify into specific requests, one being for "actions" (any observable activity). An example is the pupil pretending to kick the ball to get the adult to play football.

Agent (2.11)

A common meaning communicated at this stage is that of seeking a person to carry out an action. For example, pupils choose someone to put on their shoes, or to pour them a drink.

Object (2.12)

In addition to the labelling of objects, this covers the relationship between objects. When shown the toothbrush pupils point to their teeth, *not* to have them brushed but to show it belongs with teeth.

Attributes (2.13)

The pupils explore and communicate the properties of an object or person. For example, when playing in water they show their wet apron or they may squeeze paint through their hands to show it is slippery. An early word linked to this meaning may be "yukky".

Once the information has been gathered and sorted into the appropriate boxes the assessor is ready to make future plans. This area of Band Two is divided into five sections.

Guide to future planning

Further advice required (A)

This is the place to note if the assessor's understanding of the pupil's communication is incomplete and help is needed from other professionals.

Approach to communication (B)

Although the pupils are now active communicators, their attempts are still tentative and require the adult to follow their lead. Many pupils at this level are very active, so the adult has to follow the pupil around and join in their fleeting actions. Usually play activities are the most motivating and lend themselves easily to interaction. Appropriate play activities need to be prepared in advance so the pupil can move between them.

Teaching style (C)

Both from the assessor's observations and from personal knowledge of the pupil's level of communication, it will be clear if the adult needs to adapt the style of communication to ensure successful interaction. The following points should be considered:
- Language needs to be kept simple and relate to the activity. The pupil's level of understanding is still limited; two or three word utterances are more than sufficient.
- Questions should be avoided and a comment offered on what the child is doing or attempting to express, e.g. "That's your coat": this clarifies the meanings.
- Strategies should be planned to avoid difficult changeovers from one activity to another. Pupils at this level can become very focused on one activity and not be sure what else is being offered in its place. The use of objects of reference and a warning tone in the adult's voice accompanying the words "Soon it will be time to stop" may be helpful strategies.
- It may be necessary to create situations to encourage communication. It is always easy to anticipate needs, but doing so may prevent the pupil from using newly acquired skills. Some ideas are to place favourite toys in sight, but out of reach; to forget important routines like snacks at drink time; to ask who owns items of clothing.
- Responses from adults should be appropriate in order to motivate pupils.

Maintaining current level of communication (D)

As in Band One it is important to note the activities that can be used to maintain current levels of communicative competence. For some pupils it is unrealistic to set specific new goals but appropriate to work to maintain interaction. For these pupils, this goal can be stated on their individual educational programme. Consider the following:
- play activities that the pupil enjoys, especially if these involve an adult who can develop interactions as the opportunity arises
- situations in which the pupil is most communicative.

Goals and activities to advance communication (E)

When filling in the boxes, the assessor may have identified areas where the pupil's skills could be developed further. It may be that at home and school some different situations need to be created to encourage new meanings to be communicated.

Hearing

Vision

Physical difficulties

Medical and other problems

Pupil's name:

Date:

Verbal comprehension (2.1)

Play/"favoured activity" (2.2)

EXAMPLES: EXPLORATORY PLAY   IMAGINATIVE USE OF OBJECTS
             CAUSE AND EFFECT   PEOPLE PLAY

It is now important to observe which meanings are conveyed and how. It is from these that the first words, signs and symbol labels emerge.

Meanings communicated

Existence (acknowledges that an object or event exists) (2.3)

EXAMPLES: BY LOOKING – LOOKS AT OBJECT AND BACK TO YOU
BY POINTING – POINTS TO EVENT AND BACK TO YOU
BY VOCALISATION – VOCALISES AT PERSON AND BACK TO YOU
BY WORD, SIGN OR SYMBOL FOR OBJECT

Disappearance (comments on or requests the disappearance of a person or object) (2.4)

EXAMPLES: BY LOOKING PUZZLED AND SEARCHING AROUND FOR OBJECT OR
PERSON
BY VOCALISING THAT ACTION HAS STOPPED
BY HEADSHAKE "NO" TO INDICATE THAT A PERSON HAS GONE
BY WORD, SIGN OR SYMBOL; "BYE", "NO", "GONE"

Recurrence (requests an item to be returned or repetition of an action) (2.5)

EXAMPLES: BY LOOKING – TO ADULT AND VOCALISING
BY GESTURE – REPEATING PART OF THE ACTION
BY POINTING – POINTS TO OBJECT TO GET IT BACK
BY WORD, SIGN OR SYMBOL FOR OBJECT – "MORE", "WANT", "AGAIN"

Possession (indicates relationship between an object, person or activity to self) (2.6)

EXAMPLES: BY POINTING TO SELF WHEN ASKED "WHOSE TOY IS THIS?"
BY WORD, SIGN OR SYMBOL – "MINE", "MY GO", "ME"

Rejection (clearly rejects an object, action, event or person) (2.7)

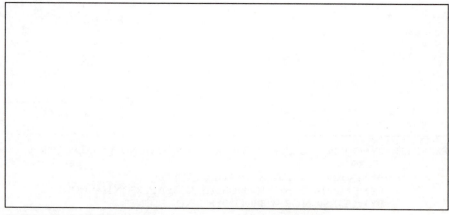

EXAMPLES: BY PUSHING AWAY PERSON   BY SHAKING HEAD
BY WORD, SIGN OR SYMBOL – "GO", "NO", "GO AWAY"

Non-existence (indicates an object does not exist where pupil expected it to be) (2.8)

EXAMPLES: HANDS EMPTY CUP TO YOU
BY SHAKING HEAD TO SHOW SHOES ARE MISSING
BY WORD, SIGN OR SYMBOL – "GONE", "NOT THERE"

Location (comments on the position of an object or person, including a request) (2.9)

EXAMPLES: BY POINTING TO A CHAIR FOR YOU TO SIT DOWN
BY WORD, SIGN OR SYMBOL – "THERE", "HERE"

Action (comments on or requests an observable activity) (2.10)

EXAMPLES: BY VOCALISING TO GIVE INSTRUCTIONS TO START AN ACTIVITY
BY WORD, SIGN OR SYMBOL – "YES", "GO", "READY"

Agent (chooses a person or object that causes an action to occur) (2.11)

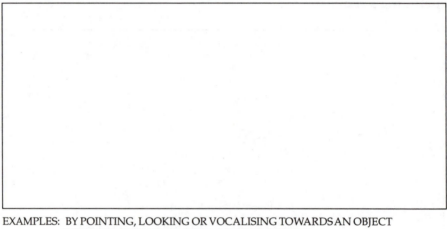

EXAMPLES: BY POINTING TO SELF OR PARTNER TO INDICATE WHO WILL DO THE
ACTION
BY LOOKING AT A HAMMER TO INDICATE THAT IT SHOULD BE USED
BY WORD, SIGN OR SYMBOL – NAMING PERSON TO CARRY OUT THE
ACTION

Object (names an object or person) (2.12)

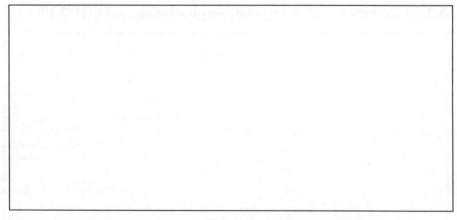

EXAMPLES: BY POINTING, LOOKING OR VOCALISING TOWARDS AN OBJECT
BY WORD, SIGN OR SYMBOL – LABELLING ITEMS

Attributes (describes an object or person) (2.13)

EXAMPLES: BY POINTING AND VOCALISING "AAH" AT PRETTY OBJECTS
BY WORD, SIGN OR SYMBOL – "PRETTY", "NOT NICE", "WET"

Further advice required (A)

Future planning

> Hearing, visual, occupational therapy, etc. (circle and specify).

Approach to communication (B)

> Describe the situation, positioning and approach which enable best interaction.

Teaching style (C)

> Describe level of language, use of eye contact, use of objects of reference, etc.

Maintaining current level of communication (D)

Goals and activities to advance communication (E)

Words, Signs and Symbols

At this level pupils are beginning to link words (signs or symbols) into sentences.

Introduction

The pupils must begin to use whatever language they have for different functions such as socialising, communicating information, initiating conversation, making requests, describing, directing, questioning and repairing misunderstandings.

Basic conversation skills become important. As pupils begin to use longer sentences for more purposes, articulation problems may become more obvious and inhibit the use of language. Speech and language therapy may help some pupils at the end of this level.

Other pupils may demonstrate a good understanding of language but have problems with expressing themselves clearly. Alternative and augmentative methods of communication may have been introduced during Band Two, the first meanings level, but should now become part of the pupil's total communication system.

Band Three is for those pupils who are able to express most of the first meanings in Band Two.

Prerequisites for the use of Band Three

Usually, this group of pupils will have progressed from their initial use of gesture and vocalisation to communicate, to the use of more formal techniques of expression such as recognisable signs and words. Total vocabulary size is likely to be around 40–50 words.

Of course many communications may still be in an idiosyncratic form, recognisable only to close family and acquaintances.

Significantly, the pupil who is ready to move to Band Three assessment is beginning to try to link ideas such as in "my coat" or "more dinner". Many pupils at this level combine several methods of expression in the same phrase, such as a gesture ("my" – points to self) and a word ("coat").

The pupil may also begin to attempt more advanced uses of language in socialising, giving new information, describing, directing and questioning.

Looking at the communications assessed in Band Three requires close observation and discussion with those who know the pupil. The following is a guide to gathering appropriate information to complete the assessment.

Gathering information

Observations

The observer should watch the pupil in different situations. It is important to distinguish between the following situations:

- The pupil communicates only through adult prompts or by answering closed questions.
- The pupil is not in a situation conducive to communication, e.g. parallel play with a silent partner.
- The pupil is relaxed with family or close friends. (This probably shows a realistic baseline of communication skills.)
- The pupil is relaxed with an adult as an active listener. (The adult should allow opportunities for initiating conversation, turn-taking, giving directions, taking time to respond and repairing misunderstandings. This demonstrates the highest level of communication that the pupil is currently achieving.)

Note the uses of communication, including first meanings, from Band Two.

Record-keeping

Keep a record of communications. It is suggested that the assessor notes communications as they occur throughout the year. Notes should be made of the means of expression for the different uses of language. Even at this level some pupils may still be using a fleeting facial expression to communicate.

Liaison with parents, carers and other staff

Once prompted, parents and carers become key contributors to both the assessment and the follow-up plans.

The pupil should be discussed with other staff who know the pupil well. It may be useful to go through the assessment boxes together with the classroom support staff.

Reference should be made to the following guidelines before completing Band Three.

Hearing, vision, physical difficulties, medical and other problems

Significant problems should be noted.

Play/(or for a much older person) "favoured activity" (3.1)

This is an important section of the assessment, giving information about the pupil's level of cognitive development and helping with the future planning. Comment should be made on symbolic and imaginative play, including sequencing of ideas.
- Does the pupil act out everyday events?
- Will the pupil make use of an adult's ideas?
- Can the pupil play co-operatively with others?
- What are the pupil's favourite play activities?

Listening skills (3.2)

As pupils respond to more linguistic input, it becomes important that they can listen. The listening skills described in this assessment were researched by Cooper *et al.* (1978).

The pupil's ability to listen continues to develop. It will depend on the complexity of the task and the pupil's motivation. The developing pattern of listening skills is described as follows.

Level 1
Highly distractible. Pupils are constantly distracted by dominant stimuli.

Level 2
Engrossed in their own activity and difficult to redirect. Pupils focus for some time on an activity of their choosing. This behaviour is rigid and inflexible and pupils have difficulty tolerating intervention or attempts to modify it by the adult.

Level 3
Can be redirected if touched or name called but not for long. Pupils at this stage are less rigid in their attention. It is still single channelled but often requires the adult to redirect it by saying the pupil's name or "Look".

Level 4
Pupils have control of their own attention. Pupils still have single channelled attention but are more able to control it. They look from speaker to task without needing the adult to "set" their attention.

Verbal comprehension (3.3)

A formal test should be completed and the results entered in the assessment box. This will clarify the comprehension level of the pupil and ensure that any spoken language used is within the pupil's comprehension.

Expressive language (3.4)

The preferred means of expression should be noted. The lists of utterances collected over the year (see "Gathering information") should be entered in this box. It is helpful if the means of expression is also recorded.

Guide to uses of communication

Guide to socialisation and conversation (3.5)

Comment should be made on how the pupil initiates conversation, responds to topics introduced by others, takes turns in conversation, keeps on topic, makes eye contact and ends conversations.

Requests 2(3.6)

Comment should be made on how the pupil requests actions, objects, people and needs.

Gives information (3.7)

Comment should be made on how the pupil conveys new information about something that has just occurred, or information about something which is very interesting to the pupil, such as a recent haircut.

Descri2bes (3.8)

Comment should be made on how the pupil describes activities, objects and people. This section includes the use of size, colour and number. Some pupils may describe an event they have watched or taken part in.

Directs (3.9)

Giving directions or instructions to another adult or pupil means the pupil has to think clearly in order to convey the message. Comment should be made on the pupil's skills in giving clear directions.

Requests (3.6)

Jane will sign for help with her milk or the door. She will point to her watch to ask when we are going somewhere.

EXAMPLES: SIGNS/SHOWS "BISCUIT"   SAYS "ME DRINK"
POINTS TO SYMBOLS – "HOME"   SAYS "GO PLAY BIKES"

Gives information (3.7)

Jane uses signs, a speech output device, some words and actions to give information, e.g. Nanny (speech output device) is coming (point to calendar) to stay (sign "house" and "sleep").

EXAMPLES: SIGNS/SHOWS "NEW DRESS"   SAYS "DADDY TO WORK"
POINTS TO SYMBOLS – "MUMMY SHOP"   SAYS "ME GO TOWN ON BUS"

Describes (3.8)

Jane has added "dirty", "new", "happy" and "dangerous" to her vocabulary of descriptive signed words. She uses more signs to describe what she is doing, e.g. "drawing", "singing", "writing" and "painting".

EXAMPLES: SIGNS/SHOWS "BIG CAKE"   SAYS "DADDY PLAY FOOTBALL"
POINTS TO SYMBOLS – "BLUE BUS"

Questions (3.10)

Note should be made of which question words are used and which are implied by facial expression, intonation or word order.

Repairs misunderstandings (3.11)

Comment should be made on the techniques used by pupils to make the listener understand the message. In addition, look at what pupils do when they do not understand. Some examples of strategies may be:

- take your hand to show you physically
- repeat themselves more emphatically
- indicate "no", and repeat themselves
- add a new sign, symbol or word to the message.

Guide to future planning

To guide the assessor's ideas this area of Band Three is divided into six sections.

Further advice required (A)

This is the section in which assessors should note that their understanding of the pupils' communication is incomplete and that help is needed from other professionals.

Teaching style (B)

As with all the bands, adults need to consider carefully their style of interaction. Pupils at this level have still only a limited grasp of language. Here are some points to remember:

- Language still needs to relate to the current activity. Abstract language is very difficult.
- While pupils can be more directed, they still communicate more effectively when their choice of activity or topic of conversation is followed.
- Past and future events are often too abstract. Symbols can now replace the objects of reference and be used effectively to help the pupil understand the routine of the day and major changes to plans.
- Use of certain language – descriptive, questioning, etc., either spoken, signed or in symbol form – may need to be incorporated into the adult's own language.

Maintaining current level of communication (C)

Many pupils with severe learning difficulties find learning formal language systems difficult. Look at situations where they are most relaxed and motivated to communicate. Pupil-directed play, the playground, puppets, simple drama and drawing may be situations in which to develop their communication systems.

Use of AAC (alternative and augmentative communication) systems (D)

Many schools use a total communication approach involving sign and symbol systems. For pupils experiencing communication problems these can offer a real bridge to spoken language or an alternative system. In this section it is important to explore exactly how the adult will use AAC. Symbols may need to be available in class, at home or on the person as their own personal system. Signing may need to be improved both at home and in the school setting. Electronically aided speech may be essential for the pupil to communicate outside more familiar settings, or to attract attention and give information.

Goals and activities to advance communication (E)

As the Band is completed, gaps in the pupil's level of skills will occur. For the pupil just entering Band Three, this is often in the giving of information and repairing of misunderstandings, while the more advanced pupil is more likely to have difficulties directing, describing and questioning.

Having identified the gaps, goals can be set to assist the pupil to achieve a higher level of performance, where, for instance, questioning may be observed only in facial expression. In this case, specific goals could be set as follows. When the pupil uses a facial expression to question, comment should be made and an example of the question form modelled: "You are asking, 'What's for dinner?'"

Intelligibility (F)

Intelligibility can be a real difficulty for many pupils with learning difficulties. In some cases direct help may be appropriate, for others improving listening skills may be all that is necessary. For older pupils this problem is often best handled by giving support in the form of augmentative communication methods. A speech and language therapist should advise on the best solution.

Band Three: the assessment

Pupil's name:

Date:

Hearing

Vision

Physical difficulties

Medical and other problems

Play/"favoured activity" (3.1)

Describe the types of play the pupil enjoys.

EXAMPLES: SYMBOLIC PLAY
SEQUENCES (several events in one game)
IMAGINATIVE PLAY (let's pretend games)
CO-OPERATIVE PLAY (with another person)

Listening skills (3.2)

Verbal comprehension (3.3)

Results of formal test and other comments.

Expressive language (3.4)

PREFERRED METHODS OF COMMUNICATION (SIGN, SYMBOLS AND WORDS)
NOTE EXACT EXAMPLES OF PHRASES AND COMBINATIONS OF SIGNS, SYMBOLS AND
WORDS. GIVE EXPLANATIONS

Uses of communication

Socialisation and conversation (3.5)

Conversation skills, including social language.

Requests (3.6)

EXAMPLES: SIGNS/SHOWS "BISCUIT"   SAYS "ME DRINK"
POINTS TO SYMBOLS – "HOME"   SAYS "GO PLAY BIKES"

Gives information (3.7)

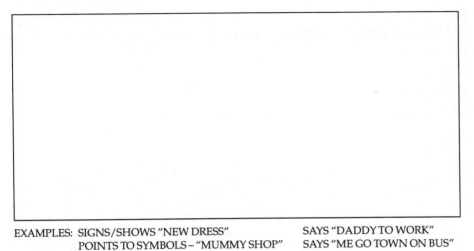

EXAMPLES: SIGNS/SHOWS "NEW DRESS"   SAYS "DADDY TO WORK"
                     POINTS TO SYMBOLS – "MUMMY SHOP"   SAYS "ME GO TOWN ON BUS"

Describes (3.8)

EXAMPLES: SIGNS/SHOWS "BIG CAKE"   SAYS "DADDY PLAY FOOTBALL"
                     POINTS TO SYMBOLS – "BLUE BUS"

Directs (3.9)

EXAMPLES: SIGNS/SHOWS "KICK BALL"   SAYS/GESTURES "GET THAT"
                     POINTS TO SYMBOLS – "GO WALK" AND THEN SIGNS "OUTSIDE"

Questions (3.10)

Describe how the pupil asks questions and in what context.

EXAMPLES: SIGNS/SHOWS "MY COAT?" SAYS/GESTURES "WHAT THAT?"
POINTS TO SYMBOLS – "GO HOME BUS?" SAYS "WHERE MY BLUE SOCK?"

Repairs misunderstandings (3.11)

Notes

Further advice required (A)

Future planning

> Hearing, visual, occupational therapy etc. (circle and specify).

Teaching style (B)

Maintaining current level of communication (C)

Use of AAC systems (D)

Goals and activities to advance communication (E)

Intelligibility (F)

Expanding Communication Skill

Introduction

Band Four is for pupils with good basic language skills. Such pupils will be linking their ideas into complex sentences and be ready for a wider range of activities in the English curriculum. The emphasis is still on language use but using language with more difficult functions such as reasoning, predicting, evaluating and planning, as well as developing better conversation skills. These are refined by adapting styles to different situations and different audiences.

As pupils enter this level so their sense of humour develops out of their initial appreciation of more concrete incongruities. Examples range from visual incongruities such as those expressed in cartoons, to concrete verbal incongruities, for example calling people funny names, to enjoying dual meanings of words and the beginnings of the understanding of puns.

As vocabulary and skills increase, pupils can spend more time on the creative use of language. This means expanding and extending language styles by telling stories, poems and drama. Language for "life skills" is important at this level, such as use of the telephone, social sight reading activities, handling money and time skills.

Prerequisites for the use of Band Four

Band Four is for those pupils who are able to link their ideas into complex sentences. "I went to McDonald's" expands to "I went to McDonald's with Mum because it was my birthday". "I don't want to paint" might expand to "I don't want to paint but I will go and play".

The pupil can express most of the meanings that are in Band Three. Understanding language is now accomplished out of context.

Some irregular grammatical features may remain, for example irregular past tense may still be present, such as "I wented". As the pupil enters this level, articulation may be a problem and require support from a speech and language therapist.

Pupils will have established most of the basic conversation skills, for example, greetings, turn-taking, making eye contact and keeping on the topic of the conversation.

Looking at the communications assessed in Band Four requires close observation and discussion with those who know the pupil. The following is a guide to gathering appropriate information to complete the assessment.

Gathering information

Observations

Suggestions for possible situations in which to observe the pupil:
- in a one-to-one situation with a familiar adult
- in a one-to-one situation with someone who is less familiar
- in a less familiar situation such as at the shops or school office
- in a group situation such as the class lesson
- in a group situation with peers, for example at playtime
- in situations that require different language uses, for example science lends itself to observing a pupil's use of planning and evaluating skills, painting to a pupil's use of descriptive skills, and English to a pupil's use of the more creative aspects of language.

Formal assessments

There are a number of formal assessments of language that can be used and add valuable information (see also p. 74):
- *Derbyshire Language Scheme* (Knowles & Masidlover 1982)
- Carrow Test for Auditory Comprehension of Language
- *South Tyneside Assessment of Syntactic Structures (STASS)* (Armstrong & Ainley 1992)
- *Reynell Developmental Language Scales* (Reynell 1977).

A formal assessment is useful to highlight aspects of language the pupil may find difficult, e.g. verb tenses.

Record-keeping

It is suggested that the assessor writes down key utterances that pupils use throughout the year in the different situations. Notes should also be made of their attempts to use other methods of communication – gesture, signing or symbols to make themselves understood. Particular note should be made of unfamiliar situations and how well they cope or what goes wrong if they do not. Notes should be made of how successful they are with those aspects of language needed outside the classroom, for example use of time, social sight reading, vocabulary, gaining information, etc.

Liaison with parents, carers and other staff

Discussion should take place with others who know the pupil well. It may be useful to go through the assessment boxes together with the classroom staff.

Reference should be made to the following guidelines before completing Band Four.

Hearing, vision, physical difficulties, medical and other problems

Significant problems should be noted.

Listening skills (4.1)

The listening skills described in this assessment were researched by Cooper *et al.* (1978).

It is important to remember that the pupil's listening skill will fluctuate according to task difficulty and environmental factors.

Level 1
Highly distractible. Pupils are constantly distracted by dominant stimuli.

Level 2
Engrossed in their own activity and difficult to redirect. Pupils focus for some time on an activity of their choosing. This behaviour is rigid and inflexible and pupils have difficulty tolerating intervention or attempts to modify it by the adult.

Level 3
Can be redirected if touched or name called but not for long. Pupils at this stage are less rigid in their attention. It is still single channelled but often requires the adult to redirect it by saying the pupil's name or "Look".

Level 4
Pupils have control of their own attention. Pupils still have single channelled attention but are more able to control it. They look from speaker to task without needing the adult to "set" their attention.

Level 5
Pupils have now achieved multi-channelled attention. As pupils work, they can assimilate new instructions while continuing their work, for example, as they are drawing, the adult says, "Add the feet". The pupils do so without stopping their work or looking up at

Guide to Assessment Band Four

the speaker. This level is considered by Cooper *et al.* (1978) to be essential to cope in a mainstream classroom.

Verbal comprehension (4.2)

The pupil has a good grasp of everyday language but formal assessment should be used to check for any problem areas, particularly of the grammatical aspects of English. Use should be made of a formal assessment such as one of those suggested in the introduction (p. 50).

Expressive language (4.3)

The methods used by pupils should be described together with any AAC they use to support their communication.

Guide to uses of communication

Gives and shares information (4.4)

Pupils at this level are able to cope with giving new and important information. This skill develops so that sharing and gaining new information can be used as a support to the pupil's learning in the classroom. Note should be made of how well the pupil copes with exchanging information.

Describes (4.5)

Pupils continue to build on their descriptive vocabulary in all aspects of the curriculum and to use it to enrich their communication. Note should be made of the variety of descriptions used.

Directs (4.6)

Pupils are capable of directing others at this level. However, opportunities need to be made to ensure that directing is done meaningfully and accurately, for example giving specific instructions to others in cookery to enable the meal to be cooked properly. Assessment should be made of pupils in both formal and informal situations where they need to use their directing skills.

Questions (4.7)

Pupils at this level are now able to use most question forms. They need to use their questioning skills to request and to gain information. Note should be made of the question forms used and the pupil's confidence in asking questions to find out new information.

Reasons and predicts (4.8)

At this level pupils are able to understand a growing number of relationships and make predictions on what will happen next. These skills are useful in decision-making and need to be fostered and developed. The classroom offers many situations to observe these skills. Observation should be made of how successful the pupil is in this area.

Plans and evaluates (4.9)

At this level pupils need to learn planning and evaluating aspects of language to organise their lives, and to judge their own success. These skills are taught in many areas of the curriculum, in particular science and technology.

Negotiates (4.10)

At this level pupils are beginning to use their language to assert themselves, to bargain for their needs against those of others, to judge others' contributions and at times to compromise. These skills are vital and can again be fostered in classroom activity, for example, in music pupils can be allowed to choose their own instrument but then be encouraged to negotiate which one best suits the particular piece of music they are producing together. Negotiating affects both peer relationships and how the individual is viewed by the group. Observation should be made of the pupil in both the informal playground situation and in the classroom where more formal negotiating will take place.

Conversation skills (4.11)

Conversation skills are important at this stage of communicative skill. They are unique to the individual.

Comment should be made on any abilities and problems apparent in this area, particular note and comment being made on the following:
- makes greetings
- is able to vary style according to the person addressed or situation, e.g. peer versus stranger
- takes turns
- ensures a contribution relates to the topic
- initiates appropriately
- knows when to use any AAC
- uses non-verbal aspects of conversation – eye contact, distance, facial expression, gesture, body language, etc.

- Repairing misunderstandings, e.g. repeating the word, adding a different word, using AAC.

Expresses feelings (4.12)

At this level pupils are beginning to express their feelings verbally. They begin by identifying their physical discomforts, "I'm cold", "I'm hungry", going on to identifying positive feelings in the phrases used by the peer group, e.g. "It's wicked". Negative feelings of anger, sadness, frustration or boredom can be more difficult to identify and to express verbally, often appearing as expletives in the first instance. Later pupils can begin to use their reasoning skills to express why they feel as they do, and this in turn can help others to find solutions to these problems.

Guide to creative use of language

As pupils develop the uses of language outlined at the beginning of the assessment, so they become ready to expand their language skills in alignment with the English section of the National Curriculum.

Speaking and listening (4.13)

- vocabulary
- speaking aloud – small group, class group, whole school
- speaking style – change of register appropriate to the listener.

Humour (4.14)

Note should be made of what the pupils find amusing and whether they attempt to make jokes (see p. xiii).

Stories and rhymes (4.15)

Listening to literature being read helps pupils to hear new vocabulary in context, to appreciate the rhythm of speech, to follow more complex sequences of events and to understand how language can be used.

Note should be made of the books (including fact, fiction and poetry) that pupils have enjoyed listening to.

Storying (4.16)

This means showing an appreciation of stories including characters, place and events. The first stage is to listen to a story and reproduce part of it by freely drawing a picture and discussing it.

Speaking and listening (4.13)

> *Alan has a wide range of vocabulary which he will use freely in a one-to-one situation with a familiar person. He will talk with the class group and is becoming more confident in speaking in front of a larger group.*

Humour (4.14)

> *Alan can see humour in many things, enjoying ridiculous events in stories and nonsense rhymes. He will laugh if he is teased or when jokes are made about what is happening in class.*

Stories and rhymes (4.15)

> *Alan really enjoys listening to stories and rhymes. This year he has enjoyed Roald Dahl stories and shorter stories where he can read some of the text himself, e.g.* The Lighthouse Keeper's Lunch.

The next stage is to try to sequence the events of a popular story.

Pupils can also attempt to develop ending of stories before trying to make a story of their own.

Notes should be made of how the pupils respond to storying activities.

Imagination and fantasy (4.17)

At this level the pupil may be involved in playing alone with small toys or drawing materials and talking through this game. It may sometimes involve another person as a listener.

Drama (4.18)

Drama provides opportunities for using and recognising different speech registers. Awareness of the appropriate language to use in different situations can be fostered through this activity. It may involve dressing up and puppets. Note should be made of the pupil's response to drama activities.

Guide to use of language for life skills

At this level pupils are beginning to need to be successful communicators in less familiar situations. To assess this, one needs to observe or discuss with the parent and others how well they succeed in some of the following situations.

Messages (4.19)

This involves giving simple messages and bringing back the answer to familiar and less familiar people.

Knowledge of time (4.20)

- explain the difference between weekdays and weekend
- use a simple timetable
- know the significance of the clock
- name the months and associate events with them
- understand yesterday/tomorrow
- understand last week/next week.

Knowledge of money (4.21)

- explain what money is for
- recognise the need for money in a shop

- match similar coins
- complete a purchase if the correct money is given
- pick out a coin by name
- recognise when change is needed
- use money without supervision when purchasing goods.

Use of telephone (4.22)

Literacy skills (4.23)

Recognising and understanding key social sight words. Some pupils will have made some progress in reading and comment should be made on literacy levels achieved.

On completing the assessment, future plans may now be made. To help with planning, this area of Band Four is divided into six sections.

Guide to future planning

Further advice required (A)

This is the place to note that understanding of the pupil's communication is incomplete. Help may be required from other professionals.

Teaching style (B)

As with the previous bands, the adults need to reflect on their communication skills. Here are some points to remember:
- The adult still needs to be aware of failures to understand, for example, the pupil may not yet have grasped a sense of time. Building timetables into the day may help this understanding grow.
- Developing negotiation with a pupil may require the adult to adopt certain management techniques for the pupil to observe and adopt later.
- As with the other levels the adult still needs to provide the appropriate model of language that the pupil is attempting to acquire.
- The adult may make good use of cognitive questioning to draw out reasoning skills.

Maintaining current level of communication (C)

It will be apparent from making the assessment that pupils at this level of communication development can best be helped by using many of the class activities to enhance communication, for example, cookery to develop planning, science to develop predicting and evaluating, English to develop creative use of language, and so on. These can then be incorporated into the lesson plans and into the pupils' individual educational plans. Particular difficulties may need to be addressed in a smaller group and subsequently built into the class situation.

Use of AAC (alternative and augmentative communication) systems (D)

Many pupils with severe learning difficulties may communicate better using AAC to support their communication. The system to be used, the person taking responsibility for it, and any further training required should be entered in this box.

Goals and activities to advance communication (E)

It will have become clear from the assessment whether or not the pupils have any gaps in their communicative skills. For pupils who are just entering this level it is recommended that the basic uses of language are developed first and then the creative and life skill uses added. How these skills are to be developed and which of the class situations are to be used should be noted.

Intelligibility (F)

Intelligibility may well be an area requiring further assistance. Advice should be sought from a speech and language therapist as to how best to support the pupil.

Hearing

Band Four:
the assessment

Pupil's name:

Date:

Vision

Physical difficulties

Medical and other problems

Listening skills (4.1)

Describe the pupil's listening skills during different situations.

Verbal comprehension (4.2)

Results of formal test and other comments.

Expressive language (4.3)

Give examples of sentences and preferred AAC systems used.

Gives and shares information (4.4)

Uses of communication

Describes (4.5)

Directs (4.6)

Questions (4.7)

Finding out information

Reasons and predicts (4.8)

Plans and evaluates (4.9)

Negotiates (4.10)

Conversation skills (4.11)

Expresses feelings (4.12)

Creative use of language

Speaking and listening (4.13)

Humour (4.14)

Stories and rhymes (4.15)

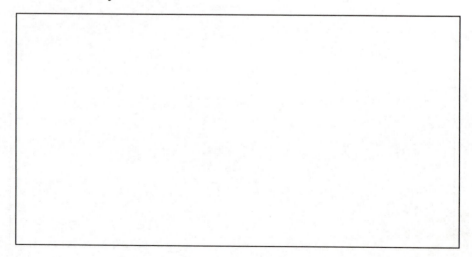

Storying (4.16)

Imagination and fantasy (4.17)

Drama (4.18)

Use of language for life skills

Messages (4.19)

Knowledge of time (4.20)

Knowledge of money (4.21)

Use of telephone (4.22)

Literacy skills (4.23)

Future planning

Further advice required (A)

Hearing, visual, occupational therapy, etc. (circle and specify).

Teaching style (B)

Maintaining current level of communication (C)

Use of AAC systems (D)

Goals and activities to advance communication (E)

Intelligibility (F)

Bibliography

Armstrong, S. & Ainley, M. (1992) *South Tyneside Assessment of Syntactic Structures (STASS)*, Ponteland: STASS Publications.

Athey, I. (1984) Contributions of play to development, in T.D. Yawkey & A.D. Pelegrini (eds) *Child's Play: Developmental and Applied*, Hillsdale, NJ: Lawrence Erlbaum.

Bloom, L. & Lahey, M. (1978) *Language Development and Language Disorders*, Chichester: Wiley.

Bruner, J. (1975) The ontogenesis of speech acts, *Journal of Child Language* **2**: 1–19.

Bruner, J. (1983) *Child's Talk: Learning to Use Language*, Oxford: Oxford University Press.

Carrow-Woolfolk, E. (1973) *Test for Auditory Comprehension of Language*, Boston, MA.: Teaching Resources (out of print).

Chomsky, N. (1965a) *Aspects of the Theory of Syntax*, Cambridge, MA: MIT Press.

Chomsky, N. (1965b) Aspects of the theory of generative grammar, in J.P.B. Allan & P. Buren (eds) (1971) *Chomsky: Selected Readings*, Oxford: Oxford University Press.

Cockerill, H. (1992) *Communication through Play: Non-directive Communication Therapy*, London: Cheyne Centre, Chelsea.

Cohen, D. (1987) *The Development of Play*, London: Routledge.

Cooper, J., Moodley, M. & Reynell, J. (1978) *Helping Language Development*, London: Edward Arnold.

Coupe, J. & Goldbart, J. (eds) (1988) *Communication before Speech*, London: Chapman & Hall.

Coupe, J., Barber, L. & Murphy, D. (1988a) Affective communication assessment, in J. Coupe & J. Goldbart (eds) *Communication before Speech*, London: Chapman & Hall.

Coupe, J., Barton, L. & Walker, S. (1988b) Teaching first meanings, in J. Coupe & J. Goldbart (eds) *Communication before Speech*, London: Chapman & Hall.

Department for Education (1993) *National Curriculum*, London: HMSO.

Donaldson, M. (1978) *Children's Minds*, London: Fontana Collins.

Ellis, M. (1973) *Why People Play*, Englewood Cliffs, NJ: Prentice-Hall.

Gerard, K. (1986) Checklist of communicative competence 0-2 years, unpublished.

Harris, J. (1974) Language communication and personal power: a developmental perspective, in J. Coupe & B. Smith (eds) *Taking Control*, London: David Fulton.

Harris, J. (1988) *Language Development in Schools for Children with Severe Learning Difficulties*, London: Croom Helm.

Harris, J. (1990) *Early Language Development*, London: Routledge.

Harrison, J., Lombardino, L. & Stapwell, J. (1987) The development of early communication: using developmental literature for selecting communication goals, *Journal of Special Education* **20**: 263–473.

Kiernan, C. & Reid, B. (1987) *Pre-Verbal Communication Schedule*, Windsor: NFER-Nelson.

Knowles, W. & Masidlover, M. (1982) *Derbyshire Language Scheme*, Derbyshire County Council.

Latham, C. & Miles, A. (1993) Putting theory into practice, *College of Speech and Language Therapists Bulletin* August, **496**: 4–6.

Leonard, L.B. (1976) *Meaning in Child Language*, New York: Grune & Strattan.

Locke, A. (1985) *Living Language*, Windsor: NFER-Nelson.

Lowe, M. (1975) Trends in the development of representational play in infants from one to three years – an observational study, *Journal of Child Psychology and Psychiatry* **16**: 33–47.

McGhee, P.E. (1979) *Humour: Its Origin and Development*, San Francisco: W.H. Freeman.

Nelson, K., Rescorla, L., Gruendal, J. & Benedict, H. (1978) Early lexicons, what do they mean?, *Child Development* **49**: 960–68.

Newson, E. & Newson, J. (1979) *Toys and Playthings*, London: Allen & Unwin.

Piaget, J. (1958) *Child's Construction of Reality*, London: Routledge & Kegan Paul.

Reichle, J. & Keogh, W.J. (1985) Communicative intervention, in S.F. Warren & A.K. Rogers-Warren (eds) *Teaching Functional Language*, Baltimore, MD: University Park Press.

Reynell, J. (1977) *Manual for the Reynell Developmental Language Scales* (revised), Windsor: NFER-Nelson.

Reynell, J. (1980) *Language Development and Assessment*, Lancaster: MTP.

Rinaldi, W. (1993) *Social Use of Language*, Windsor: NFER-Nelson.

Schweigert, L.P. (1989) Use of microswitch technology to facilitate social contingency awareness as a basis for early communication skills, *Augmentative and Alternative Communication* **5**, 192–8.

Westby, C.E. (1980) Language abilities through play, *Language, Speech and Hearing Services in Schools* **IX**: 154–68.

Resources

For further advice and support regarding the communication assessment please contact

The Redway School
Farmborough
Netherfield
Milton Keynes
MK6 4HG

Please see "communication aid centres" for information about speech output devices

British Sign Language
The Royal National Institute for the Deaf
105 Gower Street
London
WC1 E6AH

The Makaton Vocabulary Development Project
31 Firwood Drive
Camberley
Surrey
GUI5 3QD

Picture Communication Symbols (Mayer Johnson)
Winslow Press
Telford Road
Bicester
Oxon
OX6 OTS

Signalong
Communication and Language Centre
All Saints Hospital
Magpie Hall Road
Chatenham
Kent
NE4 5NG

Alternative augmentative communication resources

"To Give Them a Voice . . . "
A video introduced by Stephen Hawking
This video offers support and encouragement to anyone considering introducing speech output devices as an additional strategy for children with communication difficulties.

The Redway School
Farmborough
Netherfield
Milton Keynes
MK6 4HG

Widget Software (for Rebus symbol software)
102 Radford Road
Leamington Spa
Warwickshire
CV1 ILF

Assessments

Affective Communication Assessment
Melland School
Holmcroft Road
Gorton
Manchester
M18 7NG

Derbyshire Language Scheme
c/o Educational Psychological Service
Area Education Office
Market House
Ripley
Derbyshire
DE5 3BR

Pre-Verbal Communication Schedule (Kiernan & Reid)
NFER-Nelson Publishing Company
Darville House
2 Oxford Road East
Windsor
Berks
SL4 1DF

Reynell Development Language Scales
NFER-Nelson Publishing Company
Darville House
2 Oxford Road East
Windsor
Berks
SL4 1DF

South Tyneside Assessment of Syntactical Studies (STASS)
44 North Road
Ponteland
Northumberland
NE20 NUR